DUKE THE DEAF DOG ASL SERIES

By Kelly Brakenhoff
Illustrated by Theresa Murray

This publication was made possible in part by a grant from the West Omaha Service Club.

Copyright 2022 by Emerald Prairie Press

Photographs by Robert Chadwick of Robert Chadwick Photography

Published by Emerald Prairie Press, April 2022

Cover Design and Interior Layout by Melissa Williams Design

Supplemental video content available on www.kellybrakenhoff.com

ISBN: 978-1-7337424-7-4 (Paperback)
ISBN: 978-1-7337424-8-1 (Hardcover)

For Shelli Janning, Cathy Carotta, and the West Omaha Service Club who believed in Duke the Deaf Dog even before the first sketch.

Special thanks to my critique group: Judith Snyder, Rosalind Reloj, and Betty VanDeventer for your advice, enthusiasm, and friendship. Shout out to Colton Abendroth for the title! Thank you, Ryan Shephard for letting me borrow your dog Koa's name for Duke's friend.

—Kelly

This book is dedicated to my friends: the unconditional love and perspective shared, through tail wags (furry friends) or rich conversations (human friends). Because of you, my life is blessed.

—Theresa

Other Books by Kelly Brakenhoff

Cassandra Sato Mysteries
Dead End (Short Story)
Death by Dissertation
Dead Week
Dead of Winter Break
Scavenger Haunt (Short Story)

Duke the Deaf Dog ASL Series
Never Mind
Farts Make Noise

My best friend Koa is Deaf like me,
but we are different too.

Koa is "my dawg" because we are friends.

We have a **secret** handshake.

We both use sign language.

Sometimes Koa plays at my house.

Koa climbed really high. I stayed on the ground to help him if he fell.

I'm not afraid of **spiders**, but Koa says they're creepy.

My brother made us deputies and we searched for outlaws.

My brothers and parents can hear. Sometimes my brothers **forget** to sign so we ask, "What did you say?"

Then my brothers sign so we understand too.

Later, we **helped** make tacos.
Mom let us use all the toppings.

Koa went first because he's the guest.
I'm the host and I waited my turn.

Mom told my brothers, "Indoor voices please. You guys are too noisy!"

Our moms have rules about cleaning up messes.

Koa and I are good **cleaners**.

My dawg Koa and I love action movies. We watch TV with **captions** to know what the characters said.

My family can hear the TV, but Dad says my brothers need captions for reading practice.

Dad baked my favorite **cookies** for our snack.

We acted out superhero scenes.

I let Koa borrow my new sword.

Dad signed, "Koa's mom is here. It's time for him to go home."

Koa signed, "We didn't know the doorbell was ringing! At my house, a light flashes when someone pushes the doorbell."

I asked Mom if Koa can come to my birthday party.

Mom said,
"We will ask Koa's mom."

Sometimes I play at my dawg Koa's house.

Koa's whole family is Deaf. Koa's parents and sister sign all the time.

I understand them because I can see their signs. Even from far away.

Koa's dad and sister shot hoops with us.

Koa jumped really high!

Maybe I'll ask my dad for **basketball** shoes like Koa's.

We raced cars.
I borrowed Koa's sister's car.

We let her play with us so she wasn't left out.

At lunch time, Koa's mom flashed the lights off and on. "Time to eat!"

Koa's mom lets him cut his sandwich with a knife.

I don't like **tomatoes.**
I eat them anyway because I'm the guest.

His house has cool stuff like a video phone to call his grandma.

Everyone in Koa's family has a pillow shaker to wake up in the morning.

When my mom came, I saw the flashing doorbell light!

Our moms chatted in sign language.

Sometimes we have to **wait** a long, long time.

When my dawg Koa came over for my **birthday**, we ate cake and played games.

Koa gave me a pair of basketball shoes!

Dad bought a doorbell just like Koa's for my birthday!

My dawg Koa and I are friends.

Our houses are different.

Our families are different, but love us just the same.

Seize the Day...and Fill it with (VISUAL) Language!

By Jennifer L Cranston, M.Ed. & Doctoral Candidate at Gallaudet University

Whether a child has mild or severe hearing differences, complete access to language is critical. This is especially important during the time when a child's language develops naturally through simple exposure, which is from birth to age 5. After this optimal "window" of language acquisition, learning and internalizing language becomes much more difficult. Children with differing levels of hearing may miss some information, aka language, when relying only on auditory input (what they hear) even with assistive technology, such as hearing aids and cochlear implants. Have no fear—it is possible to remove the uncertainty and provide a *complete* language model. Make it crystal clear with visual language!

Options for Providing Visual Access to Language . . . the More the Merrier!

Type	What is it?	Examples	Time Needed to Learn	Notes
Signed language	a visual system of signs, gestures, and facial expressions with its own grammar and syntax (the rules that govern how words are organized)	American Sign Language (ASL) (Used in the US) British Sign Language (BSL) Italian Sign Language (LIS)	1-3 years for basic social interaction 5-7 years for higher/academic level skills	More than 300 signed languages used around the world!
Cued language	a system of hand shapes placed at different locations on or by the face (i.e., the side of the mouth, on the chin, on the throat/neck) to visually represent the sounds of a spoken language	Cued American English Cued Spanish Cued Arabic	10-20 hours Often taught over the course of a weekend.	The system of cueing, referred to as cued speech, has been adapted to over 75 spoken languages
Print	Written form of spoken language	Books Magazines Closed captions Labels on food Even road signs! Texting Apps	Exposure—Label everything in your house!	The written form, or spelling system, of a language is called its orthography.

No need to pick just 1!

Important Points to Keep in Mind

- New languages take *years* to learn—be *patient* with yourself!
- Provide visual access to your **home language** (and culture) *while* you learn sign language by learning to **cue** your **native language**. You are already proficient in it! That way, you won't miss the critical "window" of language development.
- Signed English and other forms of manually-coded English are not actual languages. These systems attempt to make spoken English visual but are not languages on their own.
- There are different forms of manually coded English (MCE), also known as signed English, such as SEE 1 (Seeing Exact English), SEE 2 (Seeing Essential English), CASE (Conceptually Accurate Signed English), and Pigeon Sign, which is a mixture of some signed English and some ASL.
- Manually coded English systems (MCE: SEE1, SEE2, CASE, etc.) do **not** provide access to the **sounds** of a spoken language—phonology—which are the **building blocks** of a language!
- It is **impossible** to communicate in two languages at the same time, including attempting to speak English and sign ASL simultaneously.
- Signing and talking at the same time, known as SIM COM/simultaneous communication, provides only **pieces** of the signed language and spoken language. The goal is **complete** access, so focus on one language at a time in an interaction when modeling language. For example, you could sign it *first*, *then* cue the same message (with or without your voice). You could also do this in the opposite order, just **don't mix** them. We don't want language potpourri. LOL
- Since ASL and English are *different* languages, no need to sign word-for-word of the English. Follow the structure, called syntax, of the language you are using. Syntax refers to rules of a language that dictate how words are organized, or their order.
- Languages are best modeled by *native* users. Enlist the help of Deaf individuals to expose children to proficient signed language models, especially while you are building your skills! Take advantage of the virtual world! Even if there are no local deaf native users of ASL, they can be accessed via your computer!
- Integrate language into everything you do by *"narrating life"*! Attach language to even the most mundane of routines. This "thinking aloud" provides amazing exposure to language. Ex: "It's raining outside, so I need to remember to take our umbrella!" Just make sure the language is **complete** and **accessible** to them!
- **Quality** over Quickness! Remember, speed is not important—but **complete** language access is! When learning to cue your native language or learning to sign, you may feel frustrated by having to go slower in the beginning. Take solace in knowing you are providing access to **whole** language . . . not pieces!

Resources for Further Learning

Sign language does not hinder speech development:
https://www.gallaudet.edu/gallaudets-president-cordano-dispels-the-myths-of-language-acquisition/

Language development in deaf and hard-of-hearing children:
https://clerccenter.gallaudet.edu/national-resources/info/info-to-go/language-and-communication.html

Deaf mentors:
https://cuedspeech.org/learn/start-cueing/

More support for families:
https://deafchildren.org/knowledge-center/asl-resources/sign-on/

Free ASL lessons!
https://www.gallaudet.edu/asl-connect/asl-for-free/

ASL classes:
https://deafchildren.org/knowledge-center/asl-resources/sign-on/

Learning to cue:
https://languagemattersinc.com/learn-to-cue/
https://cuedspeech.org/learn/start-cueing/

Duke the Deaf Dog My Dawg Koa ASL tutorial videos and story
https://kellybrakenhoff.com/my-dawg-koa-videos/

A Parent's Perspective by Peggy Ann Scherling

Growing up, I have enjoyed reading books and it helped me understand the importance of English. When I became a mom to a Deaf son, I wanted him to be able to understand the words he read. So, I added the labels in my house with the English words for each object such as table, chair, door, trash, and so forth with fingerspelling and a picture of the object with sign language next to it. It helped him to read the English word, fingerspelling, and sign of the word. I would also encourage him to remember how to spell the word to this object correctly. At some times, he would have to run and check it out to make sure he spelled it correctly. When we had our second son, we did the same thing, and we repeated this after our daughter came along 11 years later.

I strongly encourage the parents of Deaf and Hard of Hearing children to do the same thing because it does help Deaf children learn both languages at the same time. Not just for the children, but for the parents, too, and it's a great family activity for everyone.

A Deaf Adult's Perspective by Jonathan Scherling

Back in my childhood days, I always had books in my parents' house, but reading was not my cup of tea. My mom noticed that I was struggling to learn new words, so she came up with several innovative ideas to nurture a bilingual setting for me to keep up with my vocabulary skills. One of her innovative ideas that she came up with was to put vocabulary labels in each room at our home. These labels consisted of both words in English and drawing of a person signing. My learning style was visual and seeing these labels around the home definitely contributed to building my vocabulary development. Thank you, my dearest mommy!

A Parent's Perspective by Rebecca Willman Gernon

When I was 10 years old, my great aunt, who had worked at a school for the deaf in Chicago commented, "Deaf people don't speak, because they don't hear their language." I filed that little nugget of information away and 15 years later it proved to be one of the most valuable things I knew.

Why? Because my daughter, Amy Willman, was diagnosed as severe to profoundly deaf when she was 13 months old. As a hearing parent, I was challenged to find a way to communicate with my daughter and teach Amy why English language is needed. Reading is my passion, and I wanted her to be able to enjoy it too. By the time Amy was 2 years old, I had attached 3x5 cards with the name of the object to most items in our home, as well as on food and other items on the dinner table. This allowed Amy to see me use an ASL sign, try to lip read the spoken word, and in time to grasp that a written word is associated with everything.

The labels also taught my 4-year-old son to read at a young age. Guests to our house often wondered why we labeled toilets, closets, and other items in our home. I remember one incident when I told a rather arrogant contractor he could set up his saw in the garage. He said, "Is it through this door?" Before I could answer, his meek assistant said, "The label says it a closet."

About the Contributors

Kelly Brakenhoff is an American Sign Language Interpreter whose motivation for learning ASL began in high school when she wanted to converse with her deaf friends. Duke the Deaf Dog books have quickly become popular with children, parents, and educators for promoting inclusive conversations about children with hearing differences. She also writes the Cassandra Sato Mystery series. Kelly is a wife, mom, and grandma, and dog mom to a German Wirehair Pointer.

Theresa Murray has been creating custom art and murals for over 20 years. She pulls from her past as a grooming assistant to inspire the dog personalities for the Duke the Deaf Dog series. Theresa lives in Omaha, Nebraska with her husband, two sons, and their Westie, Tinkerbell.

Jonathan Scherling hails from the village of DeWitt in southeast Nebraska. He graduated from Iowa School for the Deaf, earned his bachelor's degree from Gallaudet University in American Sign Language and Deaf Studies in 2007, and master's degree from the University of Nebraska at Omaha in Public Administration. He has been teaching ASL/Deaf Culture at the University of Nebraska at Omaha for thirteen years. He served as President for the Nebraska Association of the Deaf for four terms. Jonathan loves being able to contribute to the community through volunteering for several organizations in Nebraska/Iowa, which helps him develop a strong sense of collaboration. He enjoys traveling, camping, exercising, playing sports and being outdoors.

Peggy Ann Skeen Scherling was born and raised in Omaha with her deaf parents. She attended Omaha Hearing School then transferred to Nebraska School for the Deaf where she graduated. She married her high school sweetheart and moved to DeWitt. They have three adult children, all of them are Deaf. While her children were young and at school, she volunteered for many groups and places. Scrapbooking and taking road trips to see her children are her greatest passions. Peggy is an avid reader, which is why she strongly encouraged her children to learn to read at an early age. She and her husband love to rescue Deaf dogs, and they are currently parents to Jory, a deaf pit-bull.

Rebecca Willman Gernon and her daughter Amy Willman co-authored *Amy Signs, A Mother, Her Deaf Daughter* and *Their Stories* (Gallaudet University Press 2012.) Gernon's manuscripts have also been published in numerous anthologies and she has penned award winning plays. She is a retired federal agent and lives in the greater New Orleans area with her husband Walt and Spot the Wonder Dog.

Amy Willman has worked as an American Sign Language Coordinator and Lecturer at the University of Nebraska-Lincoln since 2001. Before moving back to her childhood home in Nebraska, Amy taught elementary school for three years and taught ASL at Santa Fe Community College for six years. Her bachelor's degree in Elementary Level and Studio Arts is from Gallaudet University, the only Deaf university in the world. She earned her master's degree in Deaf Education from McDaniel College. Amy co-authored a book with her mother, Amy Signs: A Mother and Her Deaf Daughter, and their Stories in 2012. Amy did the ASL signs, ASL lesson and videos for Never Mind, the first book in the Duke series. She lives with her four beloved cats, three of whom are deaf.

Robert Chadwick grew up in Auburn, Nebraska, and lived in Omaha and Lincoln before settling down in Columbus, Nebraska. Photographing rock concerts has been Robert's side-profession for the last six years. He also does portrait and family photography. Robert's day job is as a Structural Civil Drafter at Nebraska Public Power District where he has worked for more than 30 years. His wife Kellie McDermott-Chadwick is originally from Florida, and they have a high-energy cat, Keanu. You can see Robert's unique photos and hire him for any special photographic projects by checking out his Facebook page https://www.facebook.com/robertchadwickphotography/. Follow him on Instagram at @rachadw66 or his online concert magazine at @govenue.

Jennifer L. Cranston has over two decades of experience working in the field of Deaf Education, having held a variety of positions, such as teacher of the deaf, ASL interpreter, cued language transliterator (CLT), as well as ASL Interpreter/CLT Supervisor and Deaf Program Specialist.

She earned her bachelor's degree in Deaf Education from Flagler College and an M.Ed. in Curriculum & Instruction ESOL from George Mason University (GMU) She is currently a doctoral candidate at Gallaudet University.

Jennifer has presented at professional conferences for twenty years and lives in the Northern Virginia area with her husband and three kids. She can often be found sporting a hoodie and surrounded by her two rescue doggos, Myla & Elsie. Myla hails all the way from the streets of Puerto Rico! (Her fur babies think their mama is cool because she's in Duke & Kao's book!)

Make a Paper Hat!

For best results use a newspaper or store sales flyer larger than a regular sheet of paper.

1 Start with newspaper folded in half the way it comes.

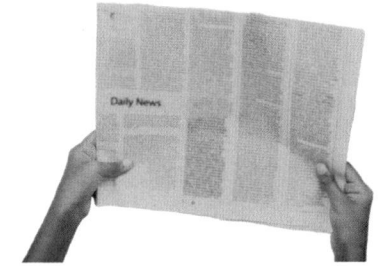

2 Fold right and left corners to the middle to form a point.

3 Open the bottom and fold up the front and back.

4 Tuck the corners over the fold to the back and front. Add tape to make it sturdy.

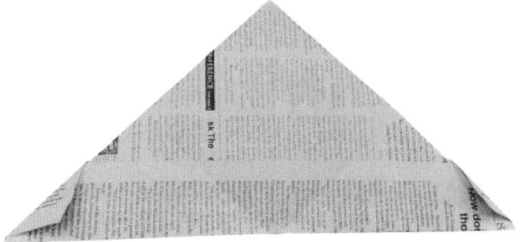

5 Open it up and shape the hat to fit your head

6 Fold up the bottom edge all around for a pirate hat.

Also works as a boat!

©2021 kellybrakenhoff.com

Made in the USA
Coppell, TX
10 June 2022